FRESHWATER FISHING

by Tim Seeberg

Content Adviser: Dr. Robert Behnke, Professor Emeritus of Fishery
and Wildlife, Colorado State University, Fort Collins, Colorado

Published in the United States of America by The Child's World®
PO Box 326 • Chanhassen, MN 55317-0326 • 800-599-READ • www.childsworld.com

Acknowledgments

The Child's World®: Mary Berendes, Publishing Director

Editorial Directions, Inc.: E. Russell Primm, Editorial Director; Halley Gatenby, Line Editor;
Susan Hindman, Copyeditor; Elizabeth K. Martin and Katie Marsico, Assistant Editors;
Matthew Messbarger, Editorial Assistant; Peter Garnham, Christine Simms, and
Kathy Stevenson, Fact Checkers; Tim Griffin/IndexServ, Indexer; James Buckley Jr.,
Photo Researcher and Photo Selector

The Design Lab: Kathleen Petelinsek, Design and Art Production

Photos

Cover: George Shelley/Corbis
Corbis: 29; Courtesy Bass Pro Shops (www.basspro.com): 8, 9, 12, 17; Jim Craigmore/Corbis:
5; Getty Images: 10, 11, 12; Todd Goppstel/Corbis: 21; Bill Howes/Corbis: 7; Phil Kelley: 13 (4);
Gunter Marx/Corbis: 22; Buddy Mays/Corbis: 27; Roy Morsch/Corbis: 24; Neil Rabinowitz/
Corbis: 25; Kim Sayer/Corbis: 6; George Shelley/Corbis: 20; Ariel Skelley/Corbis: 26; Sandro
Vanini/Corbis: 28; Karl Weatherly/Corbis: 19.

Library of Congress Cataloging-in-Publication Data

Seeberg, Tim.
  Freshwater fishing / by Tim Seeberg.
    p. cm. — (Kids' guides)
Summary: An introduction to freshwater fishing, describing basic techniques, the necessary
equipment, safety precautions, and popular places to fish.
  ISBN 1-59296-035-9 (lib. bdg. : alk. paper)
  1. Fishing—Juvenile literature. [1. Fishing.] I. Title. II. Series.
  SH445.S44 2004
  799.1'1—dc22   2003017804

CONTENTS

FRESHWATER FISHING IS FOR YOU

DID YOU KNOW THAT MORE PEOPLE

participate in fishing than in any other sport? Most fishing takes only basic equipment and a little time to learn. You don't need to know everything before you go fishing the first time. Even people who have been fishing for many years discover new things on each trip.

Fishing is about more than catching fish. It is about enjoying the outdoors. It is about the great times you will have with your family and friends.

This book is about fishing in freshwater, or water that is not salty. That means pretty much anywhere except the ocean. There are four main types of freshwater fishing: spincasting, spinning, baitcasting, and fly-fishing. This book will introduce you to spincasting and spinning, the easiest types of fishing to learn and the most popular. The basics are probably familiar to you: Using special fishing equipment and some type of bait, you try to hook a fish.

You'll probably also find that fishing hooks you!

Spending day on a lake with your family is one of the benefits of fishing.

TACKLING TACKLE

TACKLE IS THE EQUIPMENT YOU USE

to get your bait or lure to the fish. You do not need a lot of equipment to start fishing. In fact, it is a good idea to begin with basic, simple tackle.

Selecting and purchasing tackle is easy. Starter kits include everything you need to learn how to fish. The kits include a rod and **reel,** line, hooks, weights, swivels, and

A wide variety of reels are available for freshwater fishing.

some **lures.** You may want to buy some extra hooks, weights, bobbers, and swivels. The style and size of the hooks you need depend on what types of fish are in your area. The salesperson at the tackle store will know what is best to use. Buy the best equipment that you can afford.

Lures are designed to look like small fish or insects as they are pulled through the water.

The biggest differences between the types of freshwater fishing are in the rods and reels, especially the reels. Freshwater fishing tackle includes reels to store large amounts of line.

This type of reel is used when baitcasting or spincasting.

Reels let you cast a lure or bait a long distance. They also help you retrieve lures correctly, fish in deeper water, and battle larger fish more easily. Spincasting and spinning each use a different kind of rod and reel (see photos).

Spincasting tackle is ideal for beginning **anglers** because it is easy to use. A spincasting rod has a handgrip and a reel that's mounted on top of the rod's handle. You release line simply by pushing a button on the reel. Spincasting tackle is often used while fishing for bluegill, crappie, and other **panfish.**

A spinning rod has a straight handle and uses a reel that mounts under the handle. A spinning reel is often called an "open-face" reel because the spool of fishing line isn't covered. You release line using your index finger. Spinning rods and reels allow for more line to be quickly peeled off the reel, allowing you to **cast** longer distances.

Both types of reel have an adjustment called a drag that

This special reel is used for spinning.

controls how easily the line is pulled off the reel. When set correctly, the drag lets a larger fish pull some line from the reel until the fish becomes tired. Follow the directions that come with your reel to set the drag correctly.

A lure is supposed to look, move, or splash like a fish. It might also look or act like something else that a fish might like to eat, such as a worm or a crawfish. Some lures are designed to be used on the surface of water, some are made to be used a few feet below the surface, and others do their work on the bottom. The lure you use depends on what you think the fish want and how deep you think the fish are. The main types of lures are **plugs, spoons, spinners, jigs,** and plastic worms.

OTHER TACKLE ITEMS

Sinkers—Weights called sinkers are heavy pieces of metal that you attach to your line. If you are trying to catch fish at or near the bottom of a lake or stream, a sinker can get your line down to the bottom.

Bobbers—Bobbers, or floats, attach to your line to help get your lure or bait where the fish are. Bobbers float on the surface of the water, keeping your lure or bait from sinking too far.

Swivels—A swivel is used when the action of the lure, bait, or sinker will twist your line. The swivel spins to prevent the line from getting tangled.

A tackle box is the best way to keep all of your fishing gear organized.

The line used for freshwater fishing is called monofilament. It is a single strand of nylon line, usually clear, and is available in different thicknesses and strengths. If you buy a complete starter kit, your reel will probably already be loaded with line.

There are many types of hook, although you will most likely use only one or two types. The person who helps you learn to fish can tell you which types of hook you should use. You need

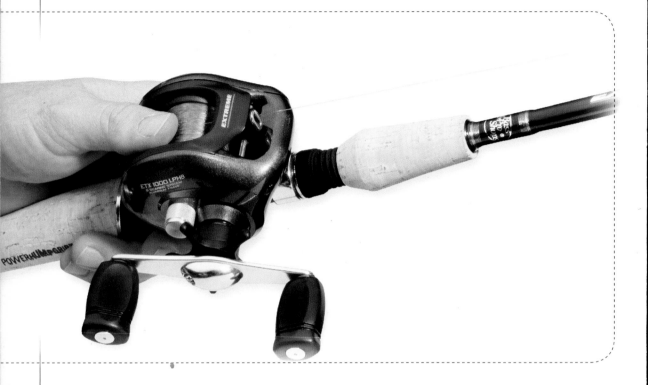

The reel attaches near the bottom end of a long, flexible rod.

to remember only one thing: Be careful! Hooks are sharp and, if not used properly, can be dangerous.

Before you can begin fishing, or even practicing your cast, you have to "rig up." Start by simply joining the pieces of your rod together according to the directions. (Some rods come in one piece. Others come apart for safety or travel.) Next, securely attach the reel. If you have a spincasting outfit, the reel goes on top of the rod. If you have a spinning outfit, the reel goes on the bottom of the rod.

Now, pull line from the reel and thread the end of the line through each of the guides (the metal rings spaced along the length of the rod). After threading the line through the guide at the tip of the rod, continue pulling it until 4 or 5 feet (120 or 150 centimeters) of line extend beyond the rod tip. Tie your lure—or your hook, if you are fishing with bait or plastic worms—to the end of your line. It is important to tie a strong knot. The Palomar knot is an easy one to tie.

If you are fishing with bait or a plastic worm, carefully push the hook through it. The person teaching you how to fish will show you how to do this. If you will be using a sinker or bobber, now is the time to attach it to your line.

Make sure you set your reel's drag properly, following the instructions that came with the reel.

TYING THE PALOMAR KNOT

- Start with plenty of line.

- Double the line and pass the end through the hook's eye.

- Tie an overhand knot (as if you were tying your shoelaces), but do not pull it tight yet.

- Pass the hook through the loop.

- Pull the loose end of the line to tighten the knot. Trim the end. Leave at least $\frac{1}{8}$ inch ($\frac{1}{3}$ cm) of your line at the knot.

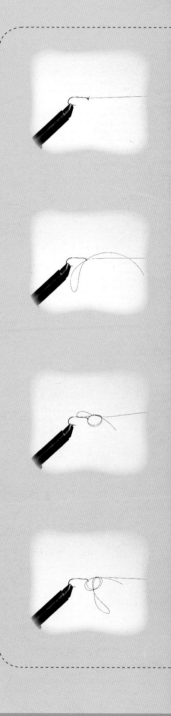

TIME TO CAST

THE WAY TO GET YOUR BAIT OR LURE

toward the fish is by casting it. Practicing your cast is an important first step to successful fishing.

Learning to cast requires a lot of space around you, but you don't need water to start practicing. The best place to practice casting is a wide-open space with short grass. For safety and to avoid damaging your lure and hooks, use a practice lure. These are rubber or plastic weights without hooks.

Now, find a spot where you can practice safely. Put a

The backcast is the first move in casting. Work with an expert to learn the proper form.

Casting forward lands the lure in the water. Practice casting until you can hit a target.

target on the ground about 25 feet (7.5 meters) away. You can use an empty soda can, a Frisbee, an old hat, or even a pine cone. Practice casting until you can consistently hit the target with your practice lure. Being able to hit a target is much more important than being able to cast a long distance. Don't be discouraged if your first casts don't go exactly where you'd planned. You will improve with practice—so keep trying! Also, learning how to use a spinning outfit may take more practice than learning spincasting.

CASTING WITH A SPINCASTING OUTFIT

A spincasting reel has a button that you push with your thumb to release the line.

1. Grasp the rod's handgrip with one hand. Push the reel's thumb button down and hold it in.

2. Face the target area with your non-casting shoulder turned slightly toward the target. Aim the rod tip toward the target, about level with your eyes.

3. Swiftly and smoothly, bend your arm at the elbow, raising your hand until it almost reaches eye level. When the rod is almost straight up, it will be bent back by the weight of the practice plug. As the rod bends, move your forearm forward with a slight wrist movement.

4. When the rod reaches eye level, release the thumb button. If the practice lure landed close in front of you, you released the thumb button too late. If it went more or less straight up, you released the thumb button too soon.

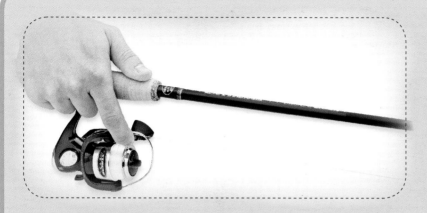

CASTING WITH A SPINNING OUTFIT

With a spinning reel, you use your finger to release the line.

1. Grasp the rod's handle, placing the reel stem that attaches the reel to the rod between your middle fingers. Place your thumb on top of the handle and extend your forefinger to touch the spool cover. With the other hand, rotate the reel spool until the **line roller** is directly beneath your extended index finger. Pick up line in front of the roller with your index finger and open the reel's **bail** with your other hand.

2. Face the target area with the shoulder of your casting arm turned slightly toward the target. Aim the rod tip toward the target at about eye level.

3. Swiftly and smoothly, using just one motion, bend your casting arm at the elbow and raise your forearm so that your hand is almost at eye level.

4. When the rod is almost straight up, it will be bent by the weight of the practice plug. As the rod bends, move your forearm forward with a slight wrist movement.

5. When the rod reaches eye level, straighten your forefinger to release the line. If the plug landed close in front of you, you released the line too late. If the plug went more or less straight up or behind you, you straightened your index finger too soon.

STAYING SAFE WHILE FISHING

The best way to enjoy your freshwater fishing experience and avoid danger or injuries is to follow these important safety tips.

Be careful when working with hooks. Hooks are very sharp. Do not cast when other people are close by. Always wear protective eyewear. Use pliers to remove a hook from a fish.

Know where you are. Wherever you are fishing, be aware of the potential hazards around you. If you're on a bank, watch where you step because boulders, logs, and holes can cause you to slip and fall. When fishing from a boat, try not to make sudden movements that will rock the boat.

Avoid sunburn. Wear proper clothing, including a hat that shades your face, ears, and neck from the sun. Be sure to wear sunscreen. When fishing, you are at greater risk of sunburn because the sun's rays are made stronger as they reflect off the water.

Protect your eyes. Wear **polarized sunglasses** to protect your eyes from the sun. They will also help you to see through surface reflections on the water so that you can spot fish more easily.

Avoid heat exhaustion. Fishing in direct sunlight on very hot days can be dangerous. You are putting yourself at risk for sunstroke. If the weather is too hot for you to stay outside comfortably, skip fishing for the day and do something indoors instead.

Avoid hypothermia. Hypothermia is dangerously low body temperature. Even on the hottest days, you are at risk of getting too cold because of the low temperature of the water around you. Stay warm and dry as much as possible. If you get too wet and start to shiver, dry off right away.

Know how to swim. All anglers should know how to swim.

LET'S GO FISHING

MOST LAKES, PONDS, RIVERS, AND

streams offer you several different places for fishing. A dock

or the bank of a river or lake are usually the safest places from

which to fish. There you can also sit and rest, and you can keep

all your gear close by. Many docks are privately owned, so first

make sure you are allowed on the dock.

A dock makes for a great fishing platform.

A quiet lake,
a sunny day, a
fishing pole: All
you need for fun!

A boat can make it possible for you to cast to water that you cannot reach from the bank and that is too deep for wading. If you fish from a boat, be sure you are with at least one person who knows about boats and fishing from boats. Do what this person tells you, and you should have a safe and fun experience. If you cannot swim, you should not go fishing in a boat. In any case, always wear a life vest in a boat.

Wherever you decide to fish, look for a weedy or rocky area where the water is several feet deep. Shallow water does not offer fish a hiding place, so you probably will not see or catch any there. The best spots are usually where the bottom changes in some way—from sand to gravel or from sand to mud. Stay quiet and avoid disturbing the water or you may scare fish away.

Now, bait your hook or tie on a lure. Cast the bait or lure as far as you can. After a few seconds, begin retrieving it. Reel in the lure slowly and smoothly, trying not to jerk it. The lure should stay slightly below the surface of the water. Pay close attention, because a fish could **strike** at any moment.

BE KIND TO NATURE

Remember, fishing is about more than just catching fish. Many people fish for relaxation or to enjoy the outdoors. It is easy to protect nature, respect other people, and still have a great time. If you see litter left by someone else, clean it up yourself. And do not leave your own trash behind. The next person to fish or walk past your spot will not enjoy it as much. Never pour liquids, especially gasoline, oil, or chemicals, into the water. You can hurt or even kill the fish.

Check your local fishing rules to see what type and size of fish you can keep. Do not use live bait (such as worms) unless you plan to keep what you catch. Fish usually swallow hooks with live bait on them, and the hooks damage their stomachs. Be considerate of the fish you catch, too. Handle them as little as possible. Some types of fish, including trout, can be seriously damaged by handling because they have very few scales. Do not squeeze any fish's gills or belly because this can damage their internal organs. Finally, remove the hook while the fish is still in the water, if possible.

FISH ON!

YOUR RIG IS PREPARED. YOU'VE FOUND

just the right fishing spot. You've practiced your casting skills.

Now comes the fun part. You send your lure out into the water,

and a fish strikes!

When a fish bites, it will probably try to swim away and

you will feel a pull on the line. Raise the tip of the rod quickly to

set the hook. If the hook sets properly, the fish will be hooked.

Fish on! A fish
strikes the lure
hard—time to start
reeling him in!

Turning the handle on the reel pulls the line—and the fish—toward your boat.

Immediately make sure you are standing in a safe place and are not in danger of losing your balance. If the fish pulls hard, let it swim away, or **run.** Check to make sure your drag is set so the fish can take line—but not too easily. When you feel the fish stop pulling, begin quickly retrieving line back onto your reel by turning its handle. Continue this give and take with the fish until the fish is no longer fighting hard to get away.

Using a net is the safest way to haul the fish out of the water.

Now, retrieve line until you have brought the fish within your reach. After bringing the fish close to you, try to keep it in the water. If you are with a person who has a net, let them scoop the fish into it.

After you have landed the fish, you need to remove the hook. Wet your hand and hold the fish firmly, but not too tightly. Use your pliers to hold the shank (straight part) of the hook. Firmly pull opposite the direction of the point of the hook. The fish may have swallowed the hook so deeply that you can't reach it with your pliers. In this case, do not try to remove it without a special hook-removal tool. You might seriously injure the fish. If the fish has sharp teeth, you also might hurt yourself.

Success! Make sure to bring a camera to capture your great catch!

It's important to remove the hook from the fish's mouth if you release it back into the water.

Removing a hook is much easier if you pinch down the small **barb** on the hook with pliers before you begin fishing. Some areas even require you to use barbless hooks. Be sure to know the rules for the water you are fishing.

Fish should never be wasted. If you catch a fish that is under the legal minimum size or that you will not use, release it quickly. If possible, keep the fish in the water and handle it carefully, pushing the hook back through the lip. You can revive a fish by gently gliding it back and forth in the water so that water runs through its gills. When it begins to struggle and can swim normally, let it go. This is called **catch and release.**

Fishing takes skill and can take practice to master. But there is nothing like the feeling of reeling in a hard-fighting fish—and then letting it go to fight another day.

TEETH + SPINES = OUCH!

A fish may be pretty and smaller than you, but do not touch it without knowing what kind of fish it is. Some fish have teeth that are big and sharp enough to cut you if you do not handle the fish properly. These include pike, muskie, and some types of salmon.

Other species have spines that can sting, cut, or puncture your skin if you are not prepared. Among the most common fish with spines are catfish, bullhead (right), and walleye.

Be sure you know it is safe to pick up the fish you have caught. Do not be afraid to ask experienced anglers for help identifying your fish. They can also demonstrate the correct way to handle it.

GLOSSARY

anglers—people who fish with a hook, or an "angle"

bail—the U-shaped part of a spinning reel that keeps fishing line from coming off the spool and also lets the line release from the spool

barb—the small piece of metal at the sharp end of some hooks

cast— to send fishing line and whatever's attached to the end of it into the water

catch and release—a practice started in the late 1930s to conserve fish populations by unhooking fish and returning them to the water

jigs—lures made of pieces of heavy metal with a hook attached that sink rapidly, letting you fish deeper in the water

line roller—the part of the bail through which the fishing line runs

lures—objects tied to the end of the fishing line to attract fish

panfish—types of fish small enough to be cooked in a pan

plugs—lures that look like a fish that other fish want to eat

polarized sunglasses—sunglasses with special lenses that block glare

reel—a spool on which fishing line is wound.

run—to pull the line out; something a fish does when it is trying to escape

set—to apply an upward motion of the rod or a quick tension on the line so that the hook penetrates the fish's mouth

spinners—lures that weigh less than plugs and spoons

spoons—usually shiny lures with a general fish shape that wobble as you retrieve them

strike—the action of a fish trying to eat a lure or bait

FIND OUT MORE

For more information about freshwater fishing, visit your local tackle store and sporting-goods stores, contact your local fish and wildlife office, and check out the books and Web site listed here.

Books

Campbell, Hugh. *Lightning's Tale: The Story of a Wild Trout.* British Columbia, Canada: Frank Amato Publications, 2000.

Mass, Dave. *Kids Gone Fishin'.* Chanhassen, Minn.: Creative Publishing International, Inc., 2001.

On the Web

Visit our home page for lots of links about freshwater fishing:
http://www.childsworld.com/links.html

NOTE TO PARENTS, TEACHERS, AND LIBRARIANS: We routinely check our Web links to make sure they're safe, active sites—so encourage your readers to check them out!

INDEX

About the Author

Tim Seeberg is a writer based in Bend, Oregon. He has a lifelong love of the outdoors and is an avid fly fisherman. A graduate of UCLA, Tim has worked in advertising and public relations, and has also written about sports history.